ZEP & HÉLÈNE BRULI

Willie...
a user's guide

Piccadilly Press • London

First published in Great Britain in 2008
by Piccadilly Press Ltd,
5 Castle Road, London NW1 8PR
www.piccadillypress.co.uk

© Éditions Glénat, 2001
Éditions Glénat, BP 177, Grenoble Cedex

A catalogue record for this book is available from the British Library

ISBN: 978 1 85340 985 1

1 3 5 7 9 10 8 6 4 2

Printed and Bound by Casterman, Belgium
Text Anglicisation by Paul Moyses
Cover Anglicisation by Fielding Design

First published in France by Éditions Glénat as *Le Guide du Zizi Sexuel*.
Written by ZEP and Hélène Bruller.

introduction

it's really important to know all about sex and private parts . . . how much **do** you know about your body and about sex? how **do** you french kiss? are walter's sperm already wearing glasses like walter? if a pregnant woman eats spinach, **does** the baby inside her eat it too? it's important to know the facts **not only** for you, but because if there's a test **on** sex and reproduction at school, you could **get good** marks.

tootuff

contents

1

being in love

what is being in love?

Even adults find it difficult to explain what being in love is. While you can 'love' your parents, your siblings, your friends and your pets, being 'in love' is very different. Most people have been in love at some point in their life. It can cause great happiness or terrible sadness – it's a very intense emotion which makes us feel alive.

What is love?

You're friends with girls and boys and everything is fine. And then suddenly there's someone who seems different from everyone else: more beautiful, more kind, more everything. They might not necessarily be a great beauty, but they are beautiful to you.

What goes on in your mind?

You may become a bit dreamy, you no longer pay as much attention to the rest of the world, and you can sometimes even lose interest in your friends a bit. This is all to be expected because your mind is totally flooded by images of the person you're in love with. You think about that person all the time. You want to see them every day and you become ridiculously overexcited when you know you are going to see them.

HEY! IT'S OK . . .

. . . I'M IN LOVE

What goes on in your body?

When you see the person you love, your heart may beat really fast. When your loved one is not around, you miss them so much that you can even get a really bad stomach ache. And some people are so moved when they see the person they love that they throw up! Feeling or acting strangely when you love someone is sometimes referred to as being 'lovesick'.

What is unrequited love?

It's when you love someone who doesn't love you, and it's hard. It can feel like your world is ending. But when you get over it – and you will – you'll understand that you weren't meant to be together, because love is best when it's returned.

Can you stop being in love?

Yes. Sometimes you suddenly realise you're not in love with that person any more, or you realise that your love has just faded away. Likewise, a person you love may stop being in love with you, which can be very painful.

Does the pain last forever?

You always think that you'll never recover, but then one day you do. All it takes is time.

Lots of boys fall in love with their teacher.

How do you tell someone you love them?

It's always quite difficult to declare your feelings. There's always the risk the person you love might reject you. But if you don't tell them they may never know – even though they may love you back. If you don't dare tell the person you love them to their face, you could always write to them or send them notes.

Can you make someone love you?

If there's one thing we can't control, it is love. There are many things you can do to try to get someone to love you, but it's impossible to make them.

Can you be in love with your cousins?

You can be in love with all kinds of people, including your cousins. But marriage between cousins is discouraged because there can be problems if you make a baby with someone who shares your genes: the baby has a higher chance than usual of having disabilities.

going out with someone

If you fancy someone (like them and find them attractive), or if you think you're in love with them, you might want to ask them out to get to know them better and see if love really does develop.

What is going out with someone?

When you fancy or love someone and they feel the same way about you, you might start going out. This is when you spend lots of time together, so you can get to know each other better. You'll also become closer and more affectionate – for instance, by kissing and touching each other.

When can you say that you're going out with some-one?

The first time you go out with someone alone is called a first date. In general, you say you are going out with someone after the first kiss. But some people just kiss for fun and don't think it means you are together. Usually a couple just know exactly when they are going out, but if you're not sure, you can discuss it together.

TOOTUFF! NADIA! GET OUT!

GREAT!

WE'RE GOING OUT TOGETHER!

10

How do you ask someone out?

Not everyone does it in the same way. A good way is to invite the person you want to go out with to the cinema or to a party with you.

Before making babies, parents went out together.

When do you kiss for the first time?

During a slow song at a party or at the end of a date, for example, you could move closer together and end up kissing. Most of the time, it's the boy who kisses the girl, but girls can certainly make the first move. Other people do it in stages: one day you hold hands, the next you are arm in arm, then you kiss each other on the cheek and finally on the lips.

How long do you stay together?

That depends! Days, weeks, months, years, forever! Sometimes you think that you're going to spend your whole life with the person you're kissing, but then they tell you to get lost after the first kiss. Fortunately, things often go better than that.

What is getting dumped?

It's when the person you're going out with says that they no longer want to go out with you. To dump someone is to break up with them.

How do you dump someone?

You can write a letter to the person you want to dump, or telephone, text or email them, but the best thing to do is to tell them face to face that you no longer want to go out with them.

IF YOU'RE IN LOVE WITH A GIRL WHO PLAYS RUGBY, IT'S EVEN MORE PAINFUL . . .

how do you kiss?

THE TENDER KISS:

THE WET KISS:

THE METAL KISS:

THE EXPLOSIVE KISS:

There are many different kinds of kiss. Tender ones, wet ones, short ones, long ones . . . Nobody kisses in exactly the same way.

How do you French kiss?

First of all, you need to place your lips against those of the person you want to kiss. Then you open your mouth and put your tongue into theirs (the person you're kissing also needs to open their mouth or it won't work). The aim is to stroke the other person's tongue with yours. And then you twist your tongues this way and that. In fact, your tongues will amuse themselves. Afterwards, you improvise.

What you should do:

- It is a good idea to tilt your head to one side, especially if you have a big nose.
- People who wear glasses can take them off
- Make sure you spit out your chewing gum first!
- You can hold hands or cuddle during the kiss.

What you shouldn't do:

- Push your tongue right into the back of the other person's mouth. The aim of kissing is not to suffocate the other person.
- Clash your teeth together: it's very unpleasant, particularly if you have braces.
- Turn your tongue around too quickly inside the other person's mouth: for the record, a tongue going round like a washing machine is not good.

Can you kiss without tongues?

Absolutely. You can kiss each other on the mouth, suck each other's lips; in short you can invent plenty of things.

Do you have to love someone to kiss them?

You don't have to love someone, but it's much better when you do, because the feelings go right to the heart.

How long does a kiss last?

That depends – it can take ten seconds or ten minutes. It's up to you. But beware of aching jaw muscles!

During a kiss, the saliva of the two people kissing mixes together.

Are there any tricks to being a good kisser?

The best trick is to want it. The more you want to kiss someone, the better you do it. To ensure a good kiss, be gentle and tender.

top pulling tips

WALK PAST WITH YOUR HEAD HIGH AND YOUR EYES FORWARD . . .

TAKE HER TO A PARTY AND MAKE HER LAUGH . . .

BUY HER A DRINK IN A COOL BAR . . .

TAKE HER HOME . . .

PRETEND THE CAR HAS BROKEN DOWN . . .

. . . DON'T FORGET THE CONDOMS.

what is puberty?

Puberty is the period of time during which you change from being a child into being an adult. It involves many changes in the body and mind, and it's not the easiest time of your life. But everyone goes through it.

When does puberty start?

When you are about 12 years old but it varies. Some people start puberty at 10, others at 16. Generally, girls start puberty a bit earlier than boys.

How do you know when puberty has begun?

Because lots of changes are happening to your body and mind.

What causes these changes?

Hormones. In the body there are glands (for example, the tonsils, the testicles, the mammary glands which are in the breasts, and sweat glands which make you per-spire). These glands make chemicals called hormones and release them into the blood to control the development of the human body. Each one has its own role.

I THINK YOU CAN REACH PUBERTY BY EATING SWEETS . . .

. . . MY BODY'S CHANGING — EEK!

BURP

There are 13-year-olds who are already taller than their parents.

Why do they call it the awkward age?

Adolescents are well aware that they're becoming adults, so they often feel they should have the same independence as their parents. And sometimes they go a bit too far (such as demanding to go out late at night without saying where they're going). Because their parents rarely agree to these demands, it can lead to arguments.

What goes on in your body?

Hormones travel around in the blood and go into many parts of the body to tell them to change. There are hormones which tell hair to grow and others that tell the breasts to swell. Hormones also tell our bones to grow. Each one has its own job. During puberty they give many orders and the body starts to change significantly.

What goes on in your mind?

When the body is changing as visibly as it does during puberty, it does not go unnoticed. The mind wonders what is going on. It can be quite distressing because you're no longer a child, but not quite an adult, either.

We call some spots 'blackheads' because their tip darkens on contact with air.

Why do you get spots during puberty?

This is yet another effect of hormones. While hormones are changing all sorts of things in the body, they sometimes temporarily increase natural bodily functions such as the secretion of oil, which prevents the skin from drying out. Too much oil blocks your pores and causes spots to appear. Lots of spots is called acne.

What can you do to avoid getting spots?

There are products you can put on your skin to dry out spots, or medicines to restrict their occurrence. But spots are a normal part of puberty. You shouldn't worry if cures do not work very well. The most important thing is to wash regularly to keep your skin healthy, and if your skin is kept clean, spots are more likely to clear up.

Why do you sweat more than usual?

It's just like getting spots – it's because your hormones are extra active. Sweat can be dealt with by washing and changing clothes every day. And also there are plenty of very effective deodorants and antiperspirants for your armpits and feet – which can be especially smelly.

And people still have sex in spite of all this?

Sex! It's the great issue of puberty! Puberty is the age when you start having sexual desires. It's also the age when the body is ready to make babies (hormones are very efficient at organising all this).

What does having sexual desires mean?

It's when you want to make love to someone you fancy.

Can a boy fancy another boy?

Yes, there are boys who fancy other boys, and sometimes, as they grow up, some might change and come to like girls. And then sometimes there are boys who like girls, but grow up to like other boys.

Is this normal?

Everyone asks themselves these questions and in time everyone finds the answer: if you allow your heart to speak, you will discover if you are heterosexual (a boy who likes girls or a girl who likes boys) or homosexual – also called gay – (a boy who likes boys or a girl who likes girls).

Can a girl fancy another girl?

Yes, it's the same for girls as it is for boys.

19

puberty for boys

During puberty, boys' bodies change. Their hair grows, their voices break and their faces become covered with spots. In short, they gradually turn into men.

Where does hair grow?

Boys start off with a patch of fluff under their noses which turns into a moustache. They then get a beard (many men shave off their facial hair) and some hair around their willies. In the end, they'll have hair under their arms, around their willies, on their faces and on their chests. Some boys will have more hair than others, and in more places, like their backs and shoulders.

Where do you get spots?

On your face and sometimes on your back and chest, but they will go away in time.

Why can you no longer sing?

A boy's voice changes during puberty to become deep like a man's. This is called breaking. At first the voice has difficulty becoming deep because the vocal cords are not fully developed. Boys whose voices are breaking cannot sing because their voice keeps changing from a high pitch to a low pitch like a yo-yo. But this doesn't last long.

Do your genitals change too?

During puberty, the willy grows longer and wider, and the testicles – also called balls – grow and begin to make sperm.

What are sperm?

Sperm are the male reproductive cells and are tiny. You cannot see them with the naked eye. Sperm come out of the end of the penis in a liquid called semen. If you look at sperm under a microscope, you will see that they have a round head (but with no eyes or mouth) and a long tail which allows them to swim. They look like tadpoles.

Where are sperm made?

In the testicles. These are two egg-shaped glands inside a little pouch called the scrotum, which is below the willy.

Do testicles make a lot of sperm?

Thousands per day! They don't live very long, so your body is always making more.

What are sperm for?

For making babies. For this to happen, the sperm must meet an egg (the female reproductive cell, also called an ovum). Puberty is therefore the age when boys can, in theory, make babies, because they start to make sperm.

Why can't boys have babies?

Because babies have to grow in a pouch called the womb (also called the uterus) and only girls have a womb inside them. But without boys' sperm, girls couldn't make babies.

Why don't boys grow breasts?

Each to their own! Girls have lots of things that boys don't have, but boys also have things that girls don't. Nature has given girls a womb for developing a baby, as well as breasts to feed them after birth.

Is there always milk in girls' breasts?

No. A woman's breasts only make milk when she has had a baby and for as long as the baby is suckling after birth.

Can boys feed babies anyway?

Not with their breasts because they don't make milk. But dads can feed their baby with a bottle, which is also good.

Do boys have periods?

No. Only girls do, because periods come from the womb and boys don't have one.

puberty for girls

Girls, like boys, change a lot during puberty. They too grow hair and get spots, but in addition they also get breasts and periods.

When do girls start puberty?

Generally when they are about 12 years old, but it varies a lot.

Where do girls grow hair?

Around their sexual organs (also known as genitals) and under their arms. But girls don't get beards or moustaches, nor do they get any hair on their chests or backs.

Does a girl's voice also break?

A woman's voice is a bit different from a little girl's because of general growth, but the change is not nearly as great as it is for boys.

HER COAT'S GOING THROUGH PUBERTY ''.

What are periods for?

They are a sign that girls are able to have babies. Before their periods they can't.

What is the womb?

The womb is a kind of pouch where a baby can grow.

How do periods work?

At the start of puberty, the womb begins to prepare a little nest to receive a baby. The inside of the womb lines itself with something called a mucous membrane which contains blood to make it softer and waits for an egg to arrive. If after about three weeks no egg has implanted in the womb, the lining is no longer useful and so the body gets rid of it. The lining becomes more liquid, like blood, and leaves the body by flowing out of the vagina (the hole between a girl's legs). When this blood flows out of the vagina it is called a period. The blood flows for about five days and when it has all gone the womb starts to line itself again and so on. Girls have a period every month.

What is an egg?

It's a tiny cell that is produced in a part of the body called the ovaries. Every month, one or more eggs leave the ovaries and fall down a small chute called the fallopian tube which connects the ovaries to the womb. This is called ovulation. Girls ovulate for about two days per month. If the egg is not fertilised by a sperm, no baby is made and the girl has her period.

How does a girl know when she gets her period?

One day she finds a bit of blood in her knickers. This is normal: it means that she is having a period.

Are periods painful?

Sometimes, before and during their periods, girls get tummy aches. This is caused by the womb squeezing itself to expel the blood. How painful it is depends on the girl. Girls are often more emotionally sensitive just before their periods and cry more easily. Some girls also get headaches.

What do girls need to do?

The first thing they need to do is avoid getting their clothes dirty. To do this, girls use sanitary towels. These are little pads that stick to the inside of their knickers to absorb the blood flow. Alternatively, they can use tampons.

What is a tampon?

It's a little tube of rounded cotton with a little string attached to one end.

Where does a tampon go?

It goes inside the vagina to absorb blood before it can flow out on to knickers.

How do you put a tampon in?

The tampon is pushed into the vagina until only the string remains outside. The first time girls use a tampon they will always be a bit nervous, so they have to relax and push it in very gently. Some tampons have an applicator which makes it easier to put them in.

How do you take a tampon out?

Just grasp the little string which is hanging out and pull gently to make the tampon come out of the vagina. Tampons need to be changed regularly because they shouldn't be left in longer than eight hours. At the beginning of a period, when there is more blood, they have to be changed more often because the tampon becomes full of blood and no longer works effectively.

EXCUSE ME, MISS, YOUR LACES ARE UNDONE . . .

At what age do periods stop?

When women are about 50 years old, their bodies stop being able to have children. The hormones that cause periods are no longer produced, so periods stop. This is called the menopause.

girls' breasts

cotton wool

mandarins

Girls who start puberty a bit later than the rest often wonder why their breasts still haven't grown while some of their friends already have a woman's chest. Since they don't have real breasts, they could try using these to make themselves a pair . . .

melons

balloons

Inside breasts there are glands but no muscles. Breasts hold their shape only thanks to the skin that covers them.

Why are girls' breasts so sensitive?

When a girl's breasts start to grow, they become very sensitive. If they get knocked, it's a bit like when a boy gets knocked in the testicles: it really hurts!

Why do girls' breasts grow during puberty?

Girls can have babies from just before they get their first period. Their breasts have to be able to store milk to feed a baby, which is why they get bigger. When women are expecting a baby, their breasts prepare to produce milk so they can feed the baby when it arrives.

3

making love

are you ready to make love?

When you fancy someone, you want to touch them, to kiss them and to cuddle them. If you love someone, as you grow older, words and cuddles aren't enough to express your feelings, so you want to make love with them.

At what age can you make love?

You start to think about it when you're quite young (sometimes around 10 years old) but often you just think about it – your body isn't ready to do it. After puberty, sexual desire becomes clearer along with bodily changes. Some people make love for the first time very early, others wait until later on. In short, there is no right age for making love for the first time, but you must remember that sex with someone under the age of 16 is illegal.

Do you have to make love?

No! You should only make love if you want to. Lots of people want to make love for the first time aged 18 or 20, some wait until they are married, and this is all normal. Everyone has their own right time.

Until what age can you make love?

Until you no longer feel like it. Some people make love until the very end of their lives, others don't.

ANYWAY, I'M NOT EVER GOING TO HAVE SEX . . . IT'S TOO DISGUSTING!

ME NEITHER . . .

. . . I'M GOING TO ADOPT SPERM

What is making love?

Making love is having sexual intercourse with someone. (See p.36.)

Why do people make love?

When you love someone, you want to tell them so. As you grow up, you also want to cuddle them and one day, when words and kisses are no longer enough, you want to make love to tell them even more strongly that you want them and want to be a part of them.

How do you know that you want to make love?

It's your body and mind that decide. The day when you are ready to make love, you feel it in your body. When the person you love touches your body and it feels like a very pleasant warmth, that's when you start to be sexually aroused. But your body can be sexually aroused without your mind wanting to make love. It's better to wait until your mind and body are both really ready.

What is a virgin?

A virgin is somebody who has not yet made love. When you make love for the first time, this is known as losing your virginity.

33

What is sexual arousal like for boys?

When a boy feels sexually aroused his heart beats faster and his breathing grows deeper. His penis fills with blood and becomes harder and harder until it points straight upwards. This is called having an erection.

Do boys have erections before puberty?

Yes. They have erections at night and in the morning, and when they feel sexual desire. They may also ejaculate – when the sperm is squirted out of the penis – while sleeping, which is completely normal; this is called a wet dream.

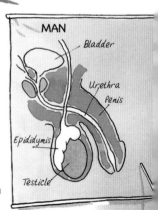

What is sexual arousal like for girls?

When a girl feels sexually aroused, her heart beats faster just like a boy's, and her breathing also grows deeper. She feels a pleasant warmth inside her and in her genital area, which is also known as the vulva. Then a small amount of clear liquid flows from her vagina.

What is masturbation?

When a boy has an erection, he sometimes feels like touching his penis and stroking it. This is masturbation.

Do girls also masturbate?

If they feel aroused, girls might also feel like stroking their genitals. But masturbating does not mean that they are ready to have sex.

What is a boy's penis like?

It is a cylinder of flesh which contains lots of blood vessels. The tip of the penis is called the glans and it is very sensitive. The tube inside the penis is called the urethra. Both urine and sperm leave the body through it.

What are testicles?

Beneath a boy's willy there is a pouch containing two egg-shaped testicles. This is where sperm are made.

What is a girl's vulva like?

It is a slit and its edges are called lips. At the top of the slit is the clitoris, which is a bit like a tiny willy, and just below is the urethra where urine comes out. Beneath this there is a hole called the vagina which leads inside to the womb. It is through the vagina that girls have sex and babies are born.

Why don't girls have testicles?

Because they don't make sperm. Girls have egg-shaped ovaries inside them that make eggs. The eggs have to meet sperm in order to make babies.

how do you make love?

Making love is the most natural thing in the world. You start by being in love with someone and wanting to hold their hand and then to kiss them. Later on, you start having sexual desires for them and wanting to be intimate. And then one day you want to make love with them. Two people who make love together are called lovers.

What is making love?

When you love someone, you want to get closer and closer to them. You start with cuddles and then you press up against one another, and you want to be even closer. To become even closer, lovers link their bodies together with their sexual organs. The boy's penis goes into the girl's vagina.

What happens?

Usually, lovers start by kissing and cuddling each other. Then they get undressed so they can cuddle each other completely naked. This is called foreplay. They carry on kissing and cuddling until they decide to make love. A boy who wants to make love has an erection. His penis becomes hard enough to enter into the girl's vagina. A girl who wants to make love feels a bit of clear liquid flow from her vagina.

YOU DO IT LIKE THIS . . .

OK, I SEE . . .

This liquid helps to make the vagina more slippery so the boy's penis can enter it easily.

How do you do it?

The boy pushes his penis into the girl's vagina. After that, the lovers start to move so that the boy's penis goes in and out of the girl's vagina.

How long does it last?

It can last three minutes or an hour! As long as they feel pleasure, the boy and girl continue to move. Then the pleasure increases until orgasm, which is the very, very strong pleasure that lovers feel at the end. The first few times, love-making doesn't usually last very long.

What does it do?

The rubbing of the boy's penis inside the girl's vagina produces a very gentle and very pleasant warmth which is called sexual pleasure.

How do you position yourself?

The boy lies on top of the girl's body. She opens her legs so that the boy's penis can enter her vagina. But you can also make love in many other positions.

Does it hurt the first time?

Girls have a small membrane of skin at the entrance of their vagina called the hymen. When they have never made love, this little barrier is usually still intact. The first time that they make love, the boy's penis opens this membrane as it enters the girl's vagina. For some girls this is a bit painful and they lose a bit of blood, but the pain is quickly surpassed by pleasure.

Why do people moan and breathe heavily?

When you feel pleasure, your heart beats faster, so you become a bit breathless. Sometimes it is so pleasurable that lovers cry out to express their happiness.

How do people have an orgasm?

As they make love or masturbate, boys and girls feel more and more pleasure. When the pleasure reaches its maximum, they have an orgasm.

What is a boy's orgasm like?

When a boy has an orgasm, semen, which is the liquid that contains sperm, squirts out of his penis: this is ejaculation.

What is a girl's orgasm like?

It's a great warmth which is very pleasurable and fills her whole body.

The Karma Sutra is a book which shows all the positions there are for making love!

Do you have to get completely naked?

Not necessarily! But it is difficult to make love with all your clothes on. When you want to make love with the person you love, you want to see them naked and to be naked yourself. The first time, it can be scary to be naked, but you can make love in the dark or with the light on, whatever you like.

Why can it be scary to be naked?

Everyone can be a bit embarrassed to be naked in front of someone. And it's quite a good thing – otherwise people would all walk naked in the streets. And also, this way, you keep being naked as a kind of present for the person you love.

What shouldn't you do?

Firstly, you shouldn't make love if you don't want to. Everyone has the right to change their mind, even at the last minute, even if they're already naked. And if you do it, the most important thing is to take your time to allow sexual arousal to rise. Sometimes boys are so desperate to make love with girls that they penetrate their lover's vagina too quickly or too strongly. This is very unpleasant for girls. The more gentle you are, the more pleasurable love-making is.

WELL, TOOTUFF . . . ARE YOU GOING TO DROP YOUR TROUSERS?

ERR . . . COULD WE TURN OFF THE LIGHTS FIRST?

Why are people sometimes afraid that their genitals aren't like those of others?

Boys can worry that their genitals are not as big or the same shapes as other boys'. Everyone is slightly different and it is nothing to worry about. Although boys can see their genitals and compare them with those of other boys, it is difficult for girls to see what theirs look like. So they sometimes wonder if their genitals are like those of other girls. It is completely normal to ask this question, and to be reassured, they can just ask a doctor.

Why can it be scary to talk about sex and love?

It is very intimate. Most people are embarrassed to talk about sex and love. It's a bit like telling a really personal secret. It's normal to be afraid of talking about it.

Who can you talk to?

You can ask someone you trust any question you like about love and sex: your parents, your big brother or sister, a friend, or another person, like your doctor.

Do you have to tell them everything?

If you have questions, you should ask them, or else you'll never get the answer. But everyone has the right to have their privacy and to keep their little love secrets to themselves.

making love

how does it work?

put your finger through here

put your finger through the hole from the other side to make the man's willy . . .

(you can also say 'sleep together')

they kiss and
take their clothes off
at the same time

(this can be tricky)

. . . by turning the page, make it **go** into the woman's hole.

don't
stop

4

making babies

how do you make babies?

When adults love each other very much, after a while they'll probably want to make a baby together.

At what age can you make babies?

From the start of puberty you are able to have babies. But having a baby is a commitment for life and you still have many things to do before you become mature enough to raise a child.

Who makes babies?

A man and a woman can have a baby by making love.

How is a baby made?

A baby is made when a sperm meets an egg.

How does the sperm meet the egg?

When a man and a woman make love, the man's penis goes inside the woman's vagina. When the man ejaculates, a small amount of semen containing sperm is deposited in the woman's vagina. If there is an egg in the woman's womb, it can be fertilised by a sperm, and it will grow into a baby.

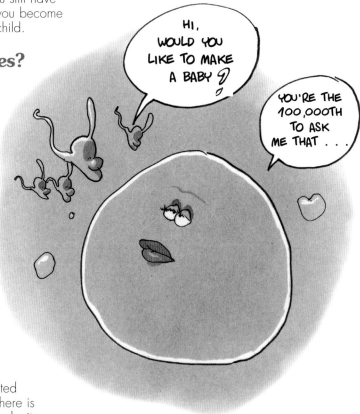

HI, WOULD YOU LIKE TO MAKE A BABY?

YOU'RE THE 100,000TH TO ASK ME THAT . . .

Why are there people who can't have babies?

Sometimes, the man or the woman is sterile. That means that they cannot have babies. The body is a very fragile system and sometimes a part of it may not work very well because of a disease or other more complicated medical reasons.

Can they have babies anyway?

Today there are ways for people who love each other to have babies even if they are sterile. Doctors can take an egg from the mum and a sperm from the dad. This little fertilised egg can be put in the woman's womb where it will grow into a baby like any other. This method of fertilisation is called 'in vitro'.

And if that doesn't work?

Sometimes you can't take an egg from the mum or a sperm from the dad. In this case parents can adopt a child who doesn't have a dad or mum. People who adopt a child raise it just like other children.

Are adopted children made in the same way as everyone else?

Of course! An adopted child was also made by a man and a woman who made love, but the child no longer has these parents. People who have adopted a child become the child's 'real' parents and love that child as much as if they'd made it themselves.

inside mum

A baby growing inside its mum leads a very busy life. And sometimes it's not the only one swimming around inside the womb . . .

How does the baby live in the womb?

The baby floats inside a sack filled with a water-like liquid called amniotic fluid. During the nine months it spends in the womb, it doesn't breathe with its lungs because there is no air. The baby receives oxygen from its mum through the umbilical cord.

What is the umbilical cord?

It's a long tube which comes out of the baby's tummy and connects it to its mum.

How is the baby fed?

It receives the vitamins and nutrients it needs to grow through the umbilical cord. That's why mums are often hungry during pregnancy: they have to eat for two people!

THE MUM EATS THE SPINACH AND WHAM! THE BABY MUNCHES THE SPINACH

NASTY!

Can there be several babies in the mum at the same time?

Yes. Two if they are twins, and sometimes more!

Why do you get twins?

Sometimes the fertilised egg divides and produces two identical eggs. These will grow into two babies who look exactly alike: these are called identical twins. And sometimes, two eggs are released from the ovaries and both are fertilised. So there are two eggs which develop into babies! But since these are two different eggs, the babies are not exactly alike: these are non-identical twins.

DID YOUR DAD SLEEP WITH A PHOTOCOPIER?

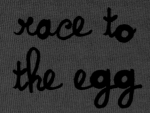

race to the egg

Sperm have to make a long journey to reach the egg. They start together in the testicles within a liquid called semen.

During ejaculation, semen containing around 200 million sperm travels through a tube called the urethra and comes out of the man's penis into the woman's vagina.

The sperm still have to swim up through the vagina and then the womb in order to reach the fallopian tubes. Their road is long and hard, and only a small number of sperm make it to the fallopian tube where the egg is. The sperm that have completed their journey are obviously the strongest of the lot.

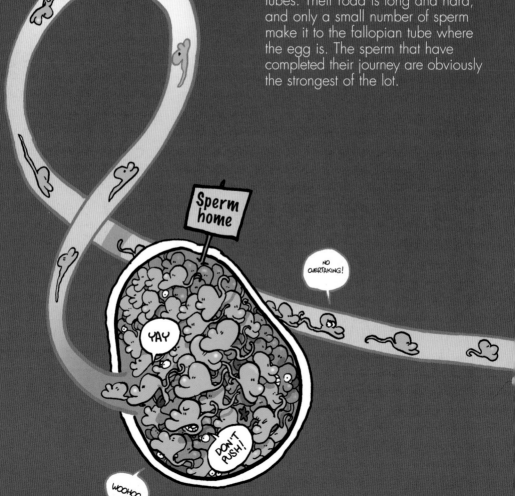

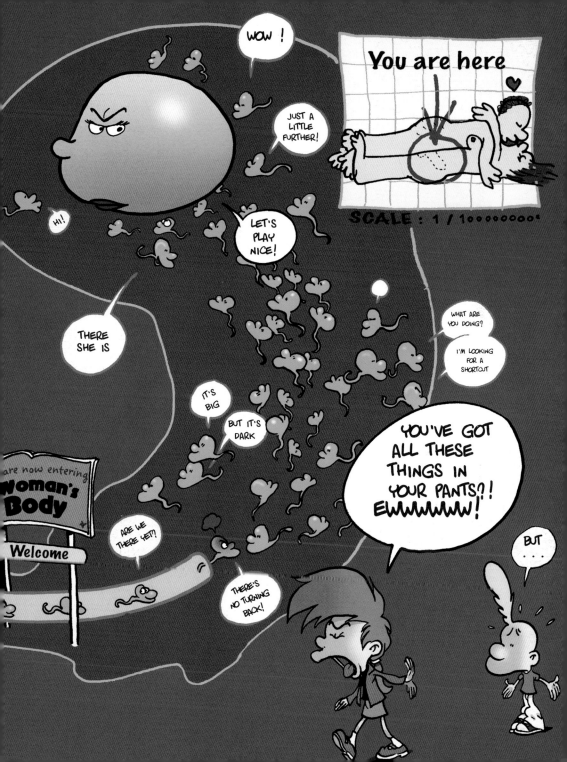

nine months

AFTER EJACULATION, ABOUT 200 MILLION SPERM SWIM THROUGH THE VAGINA AND INTO THE WOMB. ONLY 100 OR SO MAKE IT TO THE FALLOPIAN TUBES.

IN THE FALLOPIAN TUBES, THEY FIND THE EGG WHICH WAS RELEASED FROM THE OVARY.

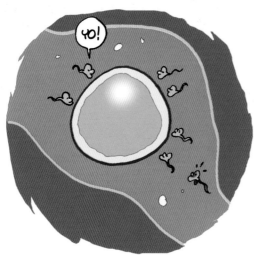

ONLY ONE SPERM CAN ENTER THE EGG TO FERTILISE IT.

THE FERTILISED EGG NOW CONTAINS
ALL THE CHARACTERISTICS OF
THE FUTURE BABY.

TO BECOME A BABY, THE EGG HAS TO DIVIDE
IN 2, THEN INTO 4, AND SO ON . . .
IT SLOWLY ROLLS INTO THE WOMB, PUSHED
BY THE HAIRS THAT COVER THE WALLS.

AFTER 8 DAYS THE EGG STICKS TO
THE WALL OF THE WOMB AND A
LITTLE NEST FORMS AROUND IT.

THE EGG NOW BECOMES AN EMBRYO. AFTER
3 WEEKS THIS EMBRYO IS JUST 2MM LONG.

AFTER 4 WEEKS, THE EMBRYO IS MORE THAN 1 CM LONG AND STARTS TO GROW A SKELETON AND A BRAIN.

AFTER 8 WEEKS THE EMBRYO IS 4 CM LONG AND HAS ALL ITS LIMBS AND ORGANS. IT HAS BECOME A FOETUS.

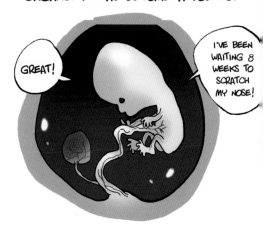

AT 3 MONTHS, THE BABY ALREADY HAS HAIR ALL OVER ITS BODY.

AFTER 4 MONTHS YOU CAN TELL WHETHER IT'S A GIRL OR A BOY.

FROM THE FOURTH MONTH ONWARDS THE MUM CAN FEEL THE BABY MOVING INSIDE HER.

AT 7 MONTHS, THE BABY USUALLY ROTATES IN THE WOMB SO THAT ITS HEAD FACES DOWNWARDS. IT WILL KEEP THIS POSITION UNTIL BIRTH . . . IT ALREADY FILLS THE WOMB COMPLETELY.

AFTER 9 MONTHS, THE MOMENT OF BIRTH ARRIVES: THE BABY LEAVES THE WOMB THROUGH THE VAGINA.

birth

After the nine months of pregnancy have passed, the baby needs to come out into the world. There are plenty of signs which show it is ready to be born.

How do you know when the baby is going to be born?

After nine months, or sometimes earlier, the mum pushes her baby out into the world. When the time comes, the mum has contractions and her waters break. These are the signs that the baby is ready to be born – also known as going into labour.

What are contractions?

This is when the tummy tenses to help push the baby out.

What happens when the waters break?

The sack which contains the liquid in which the baby was swimming breaks to allow the baby to come out. The liquid then flows out of the vagina.

How is the baby born?

The mum squeezes her tummy (a bit like how you squeeze on the toilet) to help the baby come out.

Where does the baby come out?

From the mum's vagina.

How does the baby get out?

After a few hours, the baby comes down through the vagina which widens to allow it to pass through. Then its head appears at the entrance to the vagina. Generally babies come out head-first, but sometimes they come out feet-first. This is called being born breech.

What happens after the baby comes out?

When the baby comes out it is still connected to its mum by the umbilical cord. The doctor who delivered the baby cuts this cord. A small scar will remain which everyone has on their tummy: a belly button.

I CAN SEE ITS HAIR STICKING OUT !

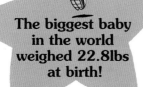

The biggest baby in the world weighed 22.8lbs at birth!

Does labour hurt?

The pain of the contractions and the baby's passage through the vagina varies from woman to woman, but the mum can be given an injection so that she doesn't feel the pain. This injection is called an epidural.

Is everybody born this way?

No. All babies grow in the mum's womb, but not all of them come out through the vagina.

Why do some mums need an operation?

Sometimes the baby cannot come out naturally because it is too big, it is not lying in the right position in the womb, or it has to be delivered before the end of pregnancy and so it is not yet ready to come out by itself. In these cases, doctors open up the mum's tummy to remove the baby directly from the womb. This is called a caesarean and it doesn't hurt because the mum's tummy is completely numbed by an injection.

Caesareans were done even in Roman times! The word actually comes from Julius Caesar, who was born in this way.

What is a baby like at birth?

A newborn baby weighs around 6–9 lbs, sometimes more, sometimes less. It is scrunched up and can barely see anything, but it can hear the voices of the people around it.

What is a paediatrician?

A paediatrician is a doctor who specialises in babies and young children.

What are hereditary genes?

The egg which grows into a baby contains coded information: this is the data which has been given to it by its parents and which makes it look more or less like them. This data also determines the features it will have, like blue eyes, brown hair and many other things.

Why are there abnormal babies?

Every egg has its own information (these little differences make every baby unique). Sometimes these differences are more unusual and give the baby a disability (like Down's syndrome). Other disabilities do not come from the information contained within the egg, but are caused by disease. Parents and specialist teachers teach these babies how to live with their disabilities.

Can humans have babies with animals?

No. It's impossible. Humans and animals don't share the same genetic code. They therefore can't reproduce together.

DON'T WORRY ABOUT YOUR EARS, BASIL, MY DATA ISN'T QUITE RIGHT, EITHER . . .

UG

maths

how are animals born?

It's not easy being a baby animal . . .
Some baby animals are born in the same way as humans (these are mammals).
Others are hatched from an egg laid by their mum (these are oviparous animals).

whales

The mother whale is a mammal.
She produces 600
litres of milk a
day to feed
her calf.

chickens

Chickens are oviparous. In order to hatch, a
chick has to break the shell of its
own egg.

snails

Snails are oviparous. They are also
hermaphrodites. This
means that a snail is
both male and
female at the same
time. As a result, a
snail can mate with
any other snail and
make babies, regardless
of whether it
is male or
female!

sea horses

The mum lays the eggs, but it's the dad who carries them around in a pouch until they hatch!

elephants

Elephants are mammals. The calf stays inside its mum for around two years before it is born!
(This is more than double the time a human baby takes!)

mice

Mice are mammals and can have as many as 15 babies at once!

kangaroos

Kangaroos are mammals. At birth, the baby is too fragile to emerge fully. So it stays in a cosy pouch on the mum's tum and drinks milk to finish growing.

queen bees

Queen bees live for 5 years. They lay about 1.5 million eggs in this time!

5

protecting yourself

what is contraception?

When two people want to make love, they don't necessarily want to make a baby. To make love without having a baby, you have to learn to protect yourself.

What is contraception?

These are the different ways you can avoid having a baby when you make love.

How does contraception work?

It works by preventing the sperm from fetilising the egg. The two most common methods are the Pill and condoms.

What is the Pill?

The Pill is currently only available for girls. It's a small tablet which contains hormones. Girls can take a pill every day for three weeks and then stop for a week to have their period.

How does the Pill work?

The hormones inside the Pill tell the ovaries not to release eggs. To make a baby, you need both an egg and a sperm, so if there is no egg there can be no baby.

What is a condom?

It's another form of contraception which is designed for boys. It's a little hood made of very fine rubber which is put on the boy's willy before love-making.

How do you put a condom on?

When the penis is erect, you place the rubber hood on top of it and then gently roll it down.

How do condoms work?

Since the penis is covered, when the boy ejaculates, the semen which comes out stays trapped in the rubber hood and so sperm cannot get into the girl's vagina to find the egg.

65

staying sexually healthy

Whether or not you have a sex life (meaning you make love regularly) you should protect your body and keep it clean and healthy.

How can I keep sexually healthy?

You should always take precautions to avoid catching diseases and to keep your sexual organs healthy and clean – it's also much nicer than smelling bad!

What is an STI?

It's a Sexually Transmitted Infection or disease which you can catch or pass on to someone else when you make love. Some can be very serious, like HIV, which leads to AIDS.

What is HIV and AIDS?

In the blood, there are microscopic cells which protect us from diseases. These cells travel around in the blood and when they find a microbe or virus that causes disease, they destroy it to prevent it from making us ill. HIV (Human Immunodeficiency Virus) is a virus which kills these defensive cells until there are no more left, at which point you have the condition known as AIDS (Acquired Immune Deficiency Syndrome). Having AIDS means that there are very few cells left to defend you when you catch an illness (for example a cold or the flu) and so the illness gets much worse and can kill you. There are new drugs that can help an HIV infected person from developing full blown AIDS.

How do you catch HIV?

HIV, the virus which causes AIDS, can be found in blood, semen and in vaginal secretions. A person who has HIV can only infect you if their blood, their semen or their vaginal secretions get inside your body. HIV cannot be transmitted through the skin or in saliva. This means that you cannot catch HIV by kissing someone, by touching them or by drinking from their glass.

EWWW!

I HOPE YOUR SEXUAL HYGIENE IS BETTER THAN THAT

How can infected secretions, semen or blood get inside your body?

When you make love with someone without using a condom, your genitals are exposed to their bodily fluids. If that person is infected with HIV, the virus can get inside your body while you are making love.

How can you protect yourself?

To avoid HIV, the only protection is to wear a condom when making love. Condoms can also protect you from other sexually transmitted infections.

What is a gynaecologist?

A doctor who specialises in girls' genitals. A girl's genitals are the parts of her body which are used to make love and to make babies and include her vagina and womb.

Why do girls go and see the gynaecologist?

After puberty, girls might start to see a gynaecologist if they have a problem with their genitals. Later on, when they are pregnant, women see an obstetrician to monitor the baby's growth in the womb.

Do boys have a gynaecologist?

No. A specialist in boys' genitals is called a urologist so if they have a problem this is who they would see.

condoms

YOU CAN GET CONDOMS FROM THE CHEMIST, SUPERMARKET OR FROM A MACHINE.

ONCE UNROLLED, A CONDOM LOOKS LIKE A THIN SOCK . . .

YOU CAN USE THEM AS WATER BOMBS . . .

OR AS SWIMMING HATS . . .

AS BUNGEE ROPES . . .

AS CHEWING GUM . . .

AND YOU CAN ALSO PUT THEM ON YOUR WILLY TO PROTECT YOURSELF.

6

watch out

watch out

When you're young, sometimes things happen which seem strange but you don't dare to talk about them. It's often difficult to ask for help when you have a problem, but you need to know that there are organisations where the people are specifically there to answer difficult questions and to protect children when necessary.

What is paedophilia?

It's an illness. A paedophile is an adult who is sexually attracted to children. Paedophiles can be very dangerous because they try to intimidate children so they can play sexual games with them. Paedophilia is absolutely forbidden and illegal. If an adult tries to touch you where you don't want them to, you should tell another adult you trust straight away.

What is incest?

Incest is having sexual desires for someone who is very closely related to you (a son, a daughter, a brother, a sister, a nephew, a niece, etc.). If a member of your family tries to touch you where you don't want them to – your genitals, for instance – you should also tell another adult you trust straight away. Generally speaking, be aware that nobody has the right to touch you if you don't want them to or if you feel that the gesture is not normal. Your body is your own. If you don't want someone to touch you, you should tell them not to: it's not wrong to say 'no', it's your right.

How do you know if a gesture isn't normal?

There are gestures of affection that everyone makes regularly which are completely normal. But if you think, even in the very back of your mind, that an adult has made a gesture which they shouldn't have, you should alert another adult. The best way to find out if something is abnormal is to ask someone.

What if I'm not sure?

Even if you're not sure, you should tell someone about it. If you don't want to talk to a member of your family, you can telephone one of the organisations which protect children, even if it's only to ask questions. The people who work in these organisations are there specifically to help you. You can call them just to find things out and you don't even have to give them your name. But never call these numbers for a joke, because if you telephone them without good reason, you might stop the person you are calling from helping another child who really needs to talk.

getting help

Here are the details of organisations
which can answer all your questions
or help you if you have a problem.

ChildLine
0800 1111
www.childline.org.uk

24-hour free confidential helpline for young
people with any problems

ChildLine Eire (run by ISPCC)
1800 666 666
www.childline.ie

NSPCC Helpline
0800 800 5000
www.nspcc.org.uk

Advice and support for any young person who
has suffered or is suffering from physical,
emotional or sexual abuse. (NB: This helpline
does not guarantee confidentiality in cases of
serious abuse, but you can ask for advice
without disclosing your name and location.
If in doubt, check with the helpline counsellor
who will always tell you at what point they
would have to break confidentiality.)

Samaritans
08457 90 90 90 (UK)
1850 90 90 90 (Eire)

24-hour confidential helpline for young people
with any problems

Sexwise
0800 28 29 30
www.ruthinking.co.uk

Confidential helpline for teenagers on sex,
relationships and contraception

Brook
0800 0185 023
www.brook.org.uk

Provides free, confidential contraception and
sex advice for young people

Family Planning Association
0845 310 1334
www.fpa.org.uk

Medical advice on contraception, pregnancy
and sexually transmitted infections

USEFUL WEBSITES

www.wiredforhealth.gov.uk
Lots of useful information about healthy eating
and other aspects of health and growing

www.mindbodysoul.gov.uk
Lots of useful information on growing up

www.avert.org
Information on AIDS, sex and contraception
and homosexuality

www.stopspots.org
Offers advice and support for people suffering
with acne

knob

cock

prick

todger

tool

wecker

trouser
snake

dong

names for a boy's private parts

It's hard...

For a boy to pee with an erection

Women who can't have a baby with their lover's sperm can get sperm from a special bank. The first sperm bank was founded in 1973.

THAT MUST BE AN AUTOMATIC DISPENSER

KILLER PUT-DOWNS

CAN I GET YOU A DRINK?

SURE, ONE FOR ME AND ONE FOR MY GIRLFRIEND . . .

In certain Aborigine tribes, a boy demonstrates his love to a girl by putting his finger in his armpit and then putting it under her nose so she can smell it.

THAT'S ROUGH!

NOT REALLY . . . YOU JUST HAVE TO PUT A CONDOM ON YOUR FINGER . . .

The Amazons were female warriors who lived long ago. They fought on horseback with bows and arrows. To avoid problems when firing, they would cut off one breast.

WERE YOU A DOUBLE AMAZON?

In the Middle Ages, a girl's private parts were called a "cuniculi", which means "little rabbit" in Latin!

There are 200 million sperm in a single ejaculation.

dick

one-eyed monster

helmet

boner

prick

member

weiner

shlang

names for a boy's private parts

In ancient times, Greek athletes exercised completely naked. The word "gymnastics" comes from the Greek "gymnos" meaning "naked".

Record for the longest kiss

approximately 30 hours non-stop!

Baby Swimmers

Babies know how to swim from birth. Today women can even give birth in a pool filled with water that resembles amniotic fluid.

In 1992, two married astronauts made love in space on a space ship

I Love You

Throughou the

French	German	Italian	Spanis
je t'aime	ich liebe dich	ti amo	te quiero

KILLER PUT-DOWNS

DO YOU WANT TO DANCE?

NO, I FORGOT TO BRING MY STEEL TOE-CAPPED BOOTS ...

Famous sumo wrestlers, who can weigh up to 300kg, are idolised by Japanese women. The bigger they are, the more they are admired.

The Biggest Bra

ever made was 15 metres long!

100% of women say they love romantic declarations

CLASSIEST MOVE: A BURPED DECLARATION

i love you

A boy's penis shrinks in cold water, or if it is exposed to cold air.

names for a girl's breasts

boobs

tits

melons

puppies

funbags

bazookas

hooters

knockers

Greek	Irish	Dutch	Swedish
s'agapo	taim i' ngra leat	ik houd van je	jag älskar dig
Arabic	**Japanese**	**Portuguese**	**Thai**
ouhibouk	ai shite imasu	eu te amo	chan rak khum
Chinese	**Polish**	**Russian**	**Turkish**
wo ai ni	ja cie kocham	ia tibia lioubliou	seni seviyorum

Top presents

A bunch of flowers

Jewellery

A box
of chocolates

A good book

A comic

A chart CD

A bottle
of perfume

A funny
gadget

Clothes

The best lovers through the ages

-100000

GMURF

-100

SPARTACUS

1100

SIR LANCELOT

Top gestures of love

Invite them to go to the cinema or to watch a video at home

Invite them to dance during a party

Hide a sweet little note in their desk

Send them a scented love-letter

Compliment them in front of their friends

Help them to cheat in tests

1650

1750

1950

2000

D'ARTAGNAN

CASANOVA

JOHN WAYNE

LEONARDO DI CAPRIO

The boy of your dreams

What type of boy will you fall for?

COOL

GROOVY

POSER

CLASSY

MUSCULAR

SENSITIVE

The girl of your dreams

What type of girl will you fall for?

FAITHFUL

TOUCHY

SPORTY

MYSTERIOUS

MATURE

UNPREDICTABLE

index

erection
34, 36, 65

feelings
9, 40

fertilisation
26, 46, 47, 55

first time
11, 32, 33, 38, 39

foreplay
36

gestures of affection
10, 72

girls
11, 16, 19, 22, 23, 24,
25, 26, 28, 34, 35, 36,
37, 38, 39, 64, 65, 67

glands
16, 21

glans
35

gynaecologist
67

hair
16, 17, 20, 24

heart
7, 13, 19, 34, 38

heterosexuality
19

HIV
66, 67

homosexuality
19

hormones
16, 17, 18, 19, 27, 64

hygiene, sexual
66

hymen
38

incest
72

twins
49

umbilical cord
54, 57

unrequited love
7

urethra
35

uterus
See *womb*

vagina
25, 27, 34, 35, 36, 37,
38, 46, 56, 57, 65, 67

virginity
33

voice (breaking)
20, 21, 24

vulva
34

willy
See *penis*

womb
22, 23, 25, 26, 35, 46,
52–55, 58, 67

big thanks to

Fabrice Le Jean

Judicaëlle Ménard

Christine Noyer

Véronique Roland

Tébo

www.piccadillypress.co.uk

☆ The latest news on forthcoming books

☆ Chapter previews

☆ Author biographies

☆ Fun quizzes

☆ Reader reviews

☆ Competitions and fab prizes

☆ Book features and cool downloads

☆ And much, much more . . .

Log on and check it out!

Piccadilly Press